THE CHURCH OF THE TRANSFIGURATION

THE CHURCH OF THE TRANSFIGURATION

Proclaiming God's Glory in Wood and Stone

MARTIN SHANNON, EDITOR

PARACLETE PRESS

Brewster, Massachusetts

Library of Congress Cataloging-in-Publication Data

The Church of the Transfiguration : proclaiming God's glory in wood and stone.
   p. cm.
  ISBN 1-55725-265-3
  1. Church of the Transfiguration (Orleans, Mass.)
  BX4603.O75 C48 2000
  271'.009744'92—dc21   00-009286

10 9 8 7 6 5 4 3 2 1

© 2000 by Orleans Church Building Foundation, Inc.
ISBN: 1-55725-265-3

Published by Paraclete Press and Orleans Church Building Foundation Inc.

Paraclete Press
Brewster MA
www.paracletepress.com

Orleans Church Building Foundation, Inc.
Orleans MA
www.cofj.net/transfig

All rights reserved. No part of this book may be reproduced in any form or by any means without the prior written consent of the publisher, except in brief quotations used in reviews.

Printed in the United States of America.

Many thanks to all those who contributed to this account of God's faithfulness, especially—

Sr. Esther Forrest
Jim Jordan
Chris Kanaga
Dick Laraja
Anna Mitchell
Sr. Irene Psathas
G. Thomas Ryan
Br. Gregory Simpson
Blair Tingley

Photographs:

Lee Andre
Dave Burnham
Br. Richard Cragg
Emily Ingwersen
Sr. Evangeline Ingwersen
Chris Kanaga
Jessica Miao
Stephen Minster

Table of Contents

Foreword ix

Introduction 3

Beginnings 5
Breaking Ground 9
A House of Prayer 15
Old Shape, New Vision 19
A Rich Legacy 25
The Art of Worship 29
The Building Sings 35
A Portal of Faith 39
Worship in Word and Sacrament 43
Living Stones 47
Called by His Name 49

Closing Page 51

Epilogue (The Future of the Project) 53

Appendix (Architects, Artists and Consultants) 55

Quicumque Christum quœritis, oculos in altum tollite:
Illic licebit visere signum perennis gloriœ.

All you who look for Christ, lift up your eyes on high,
For there you may see a sign of eternal glory.

From a hymn by Prudentius (c. 348–415) that is
sometimes used to celebrate
the Transfiguration of the Lord.

The Cornerstone was placed on the
Feast of All Saints, November 1, 1998.

Foreword

For the Lord is good and his love endures forever. His faithfulness continues through all generations. PSALM 100:5

We are happy that you have opened these pages to share our joy, for, in the words of the old gospel hymn, "this is our story, this is our song." God's love is forever, and his faithfulness is to all generations. In his mercy, he has gathered us from many places, walks of life, faiths and cultures. He always seems to take delight in working with ordinary, needy people. In turn, we have endeavored to trust him, and this seems to be the only work he has asked of us. It is that relationship of love and trust which has brought us to an extraordinary day. With hearts overflowing with thanksgiving for his love, we dedicate a place, where together, we may celebrate God's goodness. He alone is worthy to be praised.

As one abbey church, we take our place with all other Christian churches around the world, to raise our prayers and praises to the Lord, for his love is forever, and his faithfulness is to all generations. We covet your prayers as you visit and worship with us, that we may remain faithful to him in our lives and service. And, by means of this album, we invite you to share in some of our stories of God's faithfulness, to recollect with us some of the thoughts and decisions which resulted in our praising God in wood and stone.

M. Betty C. Pugsley, Prioress
The Community of Jesus
The Dedication of the Church of the Transfiguration, June 17, 2000

"The Community of Jesus calls every member to a living and growing faith in Jesus Christ. He is the source of our life, both individually and corporately. Our life together is possible only in him. We are ordinary people, called to live beyond the ordinary. By his grace, we are called out of our various backgrounds to form a living body of believers seeking to express this call in the ordinary routine of daily life."

(The Rule, Chapter I)

Introduction
TO THE COMMUNITY OF JESUS

Through the centuries, Christians have gathered to form communities in which they have supported one another in prayer, work and fellowship. In that enduring tradition, members of the Community of Jesus are joined in a common commitment of love and service to God, to each other and to the world.

On a small plot of land overlooking Rock Harbor, Massachusetts, that commitment has taken the form of an ecumenical abbey in the Benedictine monastic tradition. Members of the Community, who come from a wide variety of denominational backgrounds and occupations, make professions of commitment according to their Rule, including vows of stability and conversion of life.

Today there are approximately 160 professed members, and another sixty children and young people, who live in privately owned homes surrounding the church and the guesthouse. In addition, some twenty-five celibate brothers and seventy celibate sisters live in their respective houses (the "Friary" and the "Convent"). The beginnings of the Community can be traced to the meeting of two Episcopal laywomen, Cay Andersen and Judy Sorensen, in 1958. Their evolving prayer and teaching ministry attracted the attention and support of a small group of single women who moved to these grounds on the shores of Cape Cod Bay and committed themselves to a covenantal relationship with one another. Several families soon followed, compelled by a sense of vocation to share in this common life of prayer and work, and, in 1970, the Community of Jesus was formally constituted.

Beginnings
THE ORIGINS OF THE PROJECT

On a blustery Saturday afternoon in the autumn of 1997, more than 350 people stood and prayed in the rain on the shores of Cape Cod Bay. At the appointed time, three dozen shovels were presented, signaling the moment when every man, woman and child would turn a spade full of mud on the newly blessed site. The foul weather itself was actually a blessing, like the biblical "dew of heaven," as it would help to make the day even more memorable. The drenched gathering was made up of members and friends of the ecumenical Community of Jesus, all of whom had been looking toward this day with eager anticipation and patient faith. It was All Saints' Day, November 1, and this was the Groundbreaking Ceremony for their new church, the Church of the Transfiguration.

The journey to this event had begun ten years previously, when the Community realized that its first church, the Chapel of the Holy Paraclete, was too small to accommodate the growing number of members and guests. Built in the tradition of American Protestant meetinghouses, it was too confining to give expression to the Community's growing liturgical life. That communal, liturgical life was now calling for a new and more harmonious space.

Someone has said that worship can happen *anywhere*, but it must happen *somewhere*. The worship of God, which had been at the heart of the Community's life since its founding, developed over the years into a full daily cycle of prayer in word and sacrament. It was for the sake of "housing" this worship, within a noble and compatible *somewhere*, that the Community of Jesus embarked upon its journey of discovery.

In the spring of 1994, a committee was formed, comprised of the Prioress and several clergy, Community members, and outside consultants. The group was assigned the task of grappling with the multidimensional issues of the Community's identity and of proposing a church structure that would express the particular character of its vocation and mission.

It became immediately apparent that much more was at stake than the size of the space or the number of seats. Constructing a new church for the future was as much about asking the right questions as it was about choosing the right materials. So the questions were asked: Who are we and what do we want to become? How might a building of wood and stone "speak" the Good News? What will it say about the people who gather every day within its walls? How will it form them? How will it relate to the whole church of Christ? How will it relate to its own surroundings? Those discussions eventually led to the realization of a fundamental principle—though the Community would build the building, over time the building would build the Community. How, then, did the Community want to *build*, and how did it want to *be built*?

Certain priorities emerged at this stage. The primacy of worship was among them, but there were others, too. For example, being an ecumenical community, the Community of Jesus wanted a space that would emphasize the common bond and heritage shared by all Christians, rather than an architecture that would be identified with only one branch of the church. As a community rooted in the Benedictine monastic tradition, the Community needed a space that would strengthen communal life and be expressive of such monastic values as discipleship, conversion of life, and hospitality. And, as a community governed by the Word of God, the Community called for a space that would teach that Word and express its truth with beauty and dignity.

The committee, therefore, plunged itself into prayer, study, and discussion in order to discern the direction of the Holy Spirit. Committee members made several research trips, including some to Europe, to experience the architectural heritage of centuries of Christian worship. What they discovered was an affinity with the very early basilica-style churches of the fourth, fifth, and sixth centuries. A vision for the Church of the Transfiguration began to unfold.

The Community hired a prominent Boston architectural firm, William Rawn Associates, to take a fresh look at the existing plans, and to develop a design. Mr. Rawn had a reputation for aesthetic as well as environmental sensitivity and innovation, and had just recently completed Seiji Ozawa concert hall at Tanglewood, Massachusetts. He employed what he called a "village green concept" in order to create a contemporary expression of a monastic community and to position the church, together with all the surrounding support buildings, in its most natural and desirable location within that community. It was the selection and blessing of that site which led eventually to the Groundbreaking Ceremony of November 1997.

Breaking Ground
ALL SAINTS - NOVEMBER 1, 1997

The Service of Groundbreaking for the Church of the Transfiguration was scheduled for the annual Feast of All Saints. The church of Christ was founded upon the apostles and martyrs and, through the generations, it has been raised and shaped by the dedicated lives of the faithful people of God. It was more than appropriate, therefore, that the Community of Jesus break ground for a new house of prayer on the same day that the church recalls those who, over the centuries, have lived and died to the glory of God. The faithful of every generation are summoned, in the words of the apostle Peter, "Like living stones, be yourselves built into a spiritual house, to be a holy priesthood, to offer spiritual sacrifices acceptable to God through Jesus Christ" (1 Peter 2:5).

That morning, hymns were sung in honor of the saints, and a list of names was solemnly read—names of those members and friends of the Community of Jesus who had gone before, who had finished their race and had left the imprint of their lives. Though invisible, their "stones" were already laid upon the foundation of the new church. That afternoon, with the echo of those names still lingering in the air, spade was put to earth, and the building of the Church of the Transfiguration was begun.

Eternal and gracious God, our heavenly Father; your people from of old have built temples of worship. You have blessed them with your presence, and you have been pleased to accept the prayers and praises raised in your name. Our hearts, too, have been moved to build a house of prayer, a place where your name will be invoked day by day by a people who wish to serve and worship you in spirit and in truth. We thank you for your faithfulness in bringing us to this day, for all the way the path has led, and for the assurance that you will bring this work to a noble end. Hallow this hour with your blessing. Be with us as we begin the work and establish the work of our hands to your eternal honor and glory; through Jesus Christ our Lord. Amen.

This opening prayer for the Service of Groundbreaking was composed by the Rev. Hal M. Helms, a long-time member of the Community of Jesus and one of its pastors. His love of liturgy, his artistic gifts, and his enthusiastic interest in church architecture made him a valuable member of the Liturgy Committee from its inception. In anticipation of the Groundbreaking, he wrote this prayer in the mid-summer of 1997. Hal's name was among those read aloud on All Saints' Day, for he was called home to be with the Lord on August 15, 1997.

A QUIET REFUGE

The first official building of the Community of Jesus was Bethany Guesthouse, the former "Rock Harbor Manor" and home of one of the founding families. Behind the house stood an old carriage shed and a circular driveway, bordered on one side by a small grove of maple trees. Large at that time, in the nearly thirty years between the founding of the Community and the groundbreaking for the new church, the trees grew enormously. With the acquisition and naming of the neighboring house, Zion, the grove became formally identified as "Zion Shade Garden." It was a private place, sheltered and quiet, a cool refuge from the heat of the day, especially in the Cape Cod summer. And, beyond the garden, spreading their branches like giant welcoming arms over the driveway of Bethany circle, those hardwood hosts greeted almost every guest and retreatant who arrived on these grounds.

So, it was a bittersweet day when the shrill sound of chain saws announced the end of the maple grove. The place chosen for the Church of the Transfiguration included "Zion Shade Garden," and when preparation of the site actually began, more than one Community member shed a tear or two at the passing of these old "friends." Anticipation was mixed with sadness as, one by one, the trees came down.

But, as God would have it, death is transformed into new life, and what is cast off finds new purpose. As the trees fell that day, it occurred to one of the Brothers that some of the wood might be saved and cured, and used in a memorial of some sort. So it was that the handcrafted tables in the Scriptorium came into being. Designed and crafted by the Brothers, the tables were made from some of the finest pieces of wood milled from the old maples.

And what of the site of the grove itself? On that spot now stands "Emmanuel Chapel," a small oratory attached to the church, and the place of reservation for the eucharistic Sacrament. It is still a private place, sheltered and quiet, a cool refuge from the heat of the day.

A House of Prayer
THE LITURGICAL PROGRAM

The worship of God is the rhythmic and unceasing heartbeat that sustains and strengthens the Community of Jesus and the lives of its individual members. When the search for a fitting architectural style for a new church began in earnest, it was primarily the Community's liturgy that provided the guiding principles which would govern the building's function and meaning. The new church would have to provide for certain actions, and, even when standing empty, it would have to mean certain things, all in keeping with the Community's preeminent vocation to both live and pray to the glory of God.

Most important, the new church would need to house the eucharist and other forms of daily prayer. It would need to be the best possible space for baptisms, professions, weddings, funerals, and all of the actions which form a community into the very Body of Christ. What space would allow all present to enter into the worship in vital spirit?

The most frequent liturgy that would take place in the new church would be the Divine Office, the "Liturgy of the Hours"—the singing of psalms, hymns, readings and prayers in Gregorian chant. As with many monasteries, the Community of Jesus required enough space to seat all its members antiphonally, that is, in two "choirs," facing one another across a common central aisle. A place for the proclamation of Scripture would need to be central. Less frequently, but still daily, would be the celebration of the eucharist, the Lord's Supper. The church's shape would need to focus on the altar, providing processional space leading to it, and gathering space around it, for, as well as being a table of celebration, it is a symbol of Christ, who unites the assembly.

Finally, and in keeping with the Community's monastic identity, the church would need to welcome guests, as well as define and sometimes separate the Community membership. In the context of worship, the values of hospitality and enclosure would both need to be upheld. What architectural form, then, could best give shape to these practices and priorities?

BACKWARDS IS FORWARDS

Two harried clergymen raced from the train. From the station to the church was but a seven-minute walk, but they needed to do it faster. It had been a half-day's journey on a one-day break from the Community of Jesus' choir tour of Italy, and the return schedule left only a few short hours to see the best basilica-churches of venerable Ravenna. Products of a "golden era" sixteen hundred years ago, the churches have survived because neither the ravages of war nor the excesses of prosperity (both of which fuel stylistic adaptations) had visited themselves upon this region.

The two men from Cape Cod were members of the Community's church building committee. For the year prior, they and their colleagues had been considering the idea of a basilica style for the Church of the Transfiguration. Steeped in their local traditions of architecture and faithful to their Protestant traditions, they came to Ravenna in search of firsthand experience with this ancient architectural design. It seemed to be a God-given opportunity.

They reached the door of the church. The rice-strewn portal portrayed the church's dedication in 425 by Saint Peter Chrysologus. They saw the great donor, Galla Placidia, depicted standing to the side. This seemed a church of another time and place. What would the austere and gospel-minded pastors of Pilgrim Massachusetts say from their graves a mile from the Community of Jesus? What would contemporary donors say about a building form so ancient and so evidently pre-American?

The limousine parked out in front of the church denoted a wedding inside, so the two men paused long enough to straighten their jackets and breathe slowly before entering through the front door. As they described later, the first look at a basilica "in operation," the first feel of the shape as they stood at the back of the nave, convinced them. The direction being taken by their community was right. The vibrant elements of the basilica—peaked roof over a rectangular, colonnaded central space leading inexorably to apse and altar—needed neither explanation nor defense. This would work! For the next few years, they and their colleagues would give exhaustive and detailed consideration to the specific benefits of the basilica model and to the exact form for their own. For a moment that day, however, the two men imagined themselves in their already completed church, and the vision brought smiles to their faces.

Old Shape, New Vision
THE ARCHITECTURE OF BASILICA

Early in the planning process, it was determined that the meanings conveyed by the new church's architectural style would need to be congruent with the ethos and future of the Community of Jesus. At issue was the question of what form would best express the Community's monastic vocation, liturgical life, and ecumenical vision. Informed by these concerns for the church's appropriate function and meaning, a decision began to take shape around the idea of a basilica, an architecture bearing contemporary possibilities and deep historical roots.

Beginning in the fourth century, public assembly halls dedicated to Christian worship began to replace house-churches. This was a logical step, since our Mediterranean forebears wanted a place that signified "public assembly," and that would accommodate large groups of active worshipers. They did not want treasure houses for a distant God, with room for only a priest or two. The whole community needed to gather before the Word and the altar. Christians were already accustomed to civic basilicas (great rectangles with apses at one or both ends) for city-meetings and public business. What better shape, therefore, for the ultimate Meeting and highest public act? The basilica was a church-shape that would become the common architectural heritage of all Christians.

Before the tragic split of the church between East and West in the eleventh century, basilicas ringed the Mediterranean. Long before the Catholic–Protestant divisions and their respective reformations in the sixteenth century, the long rectangle of basilicas graced cities in such diverse places as Denmark and Portugal. Ever since, it has been a logical option for many new builders on all sides of the church. Visit Thessalonika, Greece or Trier, Germany; the ruins of Philippi or of Ostia, outside Rome; even some new communities of Corinth or Los Angeles—they all have wonderful basilicas. The pre-denominational, and therefore ecumenical, meanings conveyed by basilica were compelling.

The ancient civic-assembly-hall type of basilica, which turned into a public-worship-hall basilica, further evolved in this country. For example, the form was freshly fashioned in harmony with every Massachusetts–town's colonial-era meetinghouse. These were all simple rectangles built for the purpose of accommodating an assembly of people as they gathered in the name of God. Beyond Cape Cod and the commonwealths fostered by the Reformation, America is replete with basilicas from French and Spanish forebears. Even the long-houses of Native Americans could be seen as coming from the same human, communal response to divinity. This new and old shape would allow the clarity and proportions of contemporary architecture to find expression in a heritage both robustly Christian and deeply American.

William Rawn, the architect selected by the Community in mid-1994, was enthusiastic about the simple shapes and complex possibilities of the basilica. He and his associates would lead the design process to a twenty-first century basilica, compatible with the Nauset region of Cape Cod. Christians have redone the basilica in each era, but the Community and its architects wanted to do more than put twenty-first century touches on a venerable form. Rather, placing monastic, liturgical, and ecumenical values in the fore, they held a sort of dialogue with the basilica's ancient progenitors. How would the whole basilica be freshly conceived for this community, for this set of rites, for this maritime corner of New England? Three years of architectural work, in collaboration with historians and liturgists, musicians and pastors, generated a building for *this* place that would welcome people of *every* place, a structure at once timeless and of this very day.

The dynamic shape of the basilica at the Community of Jesus is characterized by a 55-foot-high peaked slate roof and timber ceiling, covering a large, open, rectangular nave. From the door at the west end, the room leads inexorably to a semicircular apse at the east, and to the altar sheltered within it. This rectangular space is sometimes called an assembly "hall," and it is clearly a place for liturgical action. The altar is given primary focus, the ambo (pulpit) is set in the midst of the assembly, the baptismal font stands near the door, the nave seats the entire community antiphonally for the daily chanting of the psalms, and ample space is provided for processions and gatherings.

Sloping roofs, of similar construction to the main roof, cover two parallel but lower side aisles, which run the full length of the church. Between the nave and each parallel side aisle, marches a row of fourteen twenty-foot columns and arches, over which is set a rank of translucent clerestory windows. These windows admit diffuse natural light throughout the building and further highlight the importance of the central space.

The basilica style adopted for the Church of the Transfiguration translates the language of an ancient architectural form into modern usage. It gives physical expression to the priorities that define the identity of the Community of Jesus. In addition, it was found at the planning stage that the basilica model answered the needs of other essential elements in the Community's life. For example, as the acoustician and artistic-program planners conceived the basilica, they rejoiced—it would be perfect for both the sounds and the images that help shape a Christian assembly. The Community knew that music, preaching, and the visual environment are not plush "extras." They are constitutive aspects of the liturgical action for a people at worship.

MORNING SERENADER

From the day construction actually began, the Community has offered prayers on behalf of those working on the site. A project of this magnitude requires skilled labor of many kinds, and has involved hundreds of men and women over the past three years. In support of their work and for the sake of their safety, prayers have been made at every daily Eucharist and in every home of the Community. It is not surprising, then, that stories from their lives would be shared with Community members from time to time, during coffee breaks and other meeting opportunities.

One man began working on the site with the concrete company that poured the foundation for the church. The foundation was completed after a few months, but he was reluctant to leave. He actually changed jobs, going to work with the stonemasons, so that he could remain on the project until its completion. In a conversation with one of the Community's site managers, he disclosed that a spiritual side to his life, a side that had lain dormant for years, was awakening once again, thanks to those who were praying for him and for the safety of all his fellow workers.

Another man, who had barely spoken a word and stayed pretty much to himself each day, said as much with the look in his face as he did with his words on the day he completed his job. Before leaving, he approached one of the Community men. Tears filled his eyes as he tried to say how much working on the site had meant to him. He'd labored to build all kinds of buildings over his many years, he said, but nothing had touched him so deeply as his work on this church. He expected to further express his gratitude for the opportunity when he returned with his family, not to work, but to worship.

"The morning serenader," as he came to be nicknamed by the Sisters, discovered a particularly creative way to spend maximum time on the site. At the strike of six o'clock every morning, the rich strains of Italian arias would echo over the Common, coming from somewhere in the new church. The source was soon discovered. One of the men, arriving before the official work day began, set up a little shaving station within the newly poured, and very resonant, concrete walls. With a mirror dangling from a wire and his razor in hand, he started the day with a song and a shave, in the house of God rather than at home.

A Rich Legacy
THE ROOTS OF THE ART PROGRAM

To stand today in the Church of the Transfiguration is, in some sense, to stand in two places at once, for the rich legacy left by centuries-old churches is living and present in this modern building. Many churches that remain from the first centuries of Christian worship still contain precious artistic traces of their history. Segments of mosaic lie preserved on ancient floors or sparkle from apses overhead; colored windows gleam in the sunlight; faded frescoes still softly emerge from sanctuary and clerestory walls. Preserved either intact or in fragments, these images witness to a past generation's vision and faithfulness.

Today, walking through these churches, one feels connected with the faithful who built them and inspired by the example of faith which they expressed in doing so. Contemporary to their own time, these "saints of old" produced works of art which spoke (and still speak) of things eternal. The great salvation themes are there: the creation of the world; the formation of the covenanted people of Israel; the message of the prophets; the life, death and resurrection of Christ; visions of paradise. Portrayed in line and color, the history of God's mighty acts is recounted, and the familiar stories are told of his persistent interaction with the people he created and redeemed. And, woven into these great themes, are smaller, identifying marks of each local community in which these churches were raised—indigenous flora and wildlife; regional landmarks and buildings; the imaged faces of local personalities; the fathers and mothers in the faith. The unique identities of these early Christian communities are preserved in the buildings that they built.

These early Christian churches, with their well worn steps and remnants of art, are tangible witnesses, still comprehensible today. The stream of tradition they represent carries understanding as well as form. The pictorial language is still legible, for tradition provides common visual rules—a "canon in color"—for telling salvation's story, so that generation after generation, in every corner of the world, can always recognize the truths that are being portrayed. Without directly copying the art of the past, every age has developed new styles that respect those artistic forms and advance the essential testimony of the faith. To stand in the Church of the Transfiguration, then, is to stand within a contemporary expression of an age-old tradition.

SOME GREAT COMMISSIONS

The commissioning of artists and artisans has resulted in a collaborative enterprise by a team of specialists in their respective fields. Even now, with the ongoing development of the artistic program of the church, that team continues to grow. And, along the way, there have been some very happy encounters.

In the winter of 1994, the Liturgy Committee made a research trip to Europe, accompanied by the architects and consultants. The primary goal was to experience various church buildings in their contexts and the effect of the art, iconography, and liturgical furnishings within them. It was during a brief stay in Ravenna, Italy, that the committee met Alessandra Caprara, of the *Mosaici Antichi e Moderni*. Walking through her mosaic studio and admiring her work, they began almost immediately to wonder what role she might play in creating mosaics for the Church of the Transfiguration. What was intended to be only a "sidetrip" ultimately resulted in Alessandra's thorough immersion in the project.

The elements of the church requiring stone carving presented a unique and ambitious challenge. Régis Demange brought his exceptional skill as well as a touch of French influence to the church when he signed on to the project. He also brought a considerable degree of commitment. To best accomplish the task, he and his wife actually moved from California and took up residence in the Community's neighboring town of Brewster.

Beholding the west door is destined to be, for most people, their first experience of the church. The planned artistic program needed to be realized with this special consideration in mind. Having heard of the project, Romolo Del Deo submitted an approach that was immediately embraced by the committee. In fact, his particular style, which draws upon his training in Florence, Italy, needed representation in the new church. It was a fringe benefit when the committee discovered that they had hired a native of Provincetown, Massachusetts, and one of Cape Cod's own.

Among the design submissions made for the

face of Christ in the apse, one in particular stood out for its strength and vibrancy. It turned out that, in order to produce that submission, and without any assurance of its acceptance, this artist had declined a secure job offer in Saudi Arabia in the hopes that she might become a part of the project.

The attraction to Helen McLean's work was unanimous. What's more, upon reading her materials and seeing more of her work, the committee realized that in selecting her, they had ensured the inclusion of the Celtic tradition among all those represented in the church's art program.

The Art of Worship
A PROGRAM OF IMAGES AND FORMS

With the aid of liturgical and artistic consultants, the art program for the Church of the Transfiguration began to develop in close association with the architecture. The building and its art work were considered in relation to the liturgical action that would take place within the space. The iconographic program would complement the liturgy, to express visually the history of humanity's salvation. An Art Program Committee worked diligently to determine what stories to tell, as well as where and how they should be depicted. A sense of hierarchy of images was established in order to maintain visual balance, unity, and focus. One principle was predominant in all this planning. Even when standing empty, the building should speak. Visually, it must teach the gospel.

That teaching begins with the exterior of the building. The use of limestone blocks for the construction symbolizes Jesus Christ as the "Rock" of salvation and at the same time achieves a sense of permanence and strength. Harmony with the natural surroundings of Cape Cod is accomplished through the warm, sandy color. It is almost as if the church rises up out of the earth. Placed behind each stone, and set as permanent prayer memorials within the walls of the church, are the names of Community members, friends, families and benefactors. Though unseen, these markers give a voice of thanksgiving to each stone.

The bronze door at the west end of the church depicts the sixth day of creation. Adam and Eve, freshly inspired by the breath of the Spirit, are presented flanking the Tree of Life. They admit the worshiper across a threshold, from the sights of creation into a space which points to the new creation in Christ.

The baptismal font, with its eight sides and mosaic floor, represents the initial step into salvation. It sits just beyond the door, serving as the gateway to the nave. The ambo, a platform and reading desk for proclaiming the Scriptures, is located farther down the nave, on the same central axis, as a reminder that the Word of God stands central to the life of the church. Finally, the altar, the table of the Lord's Supper, stands at the apex of this processional pathway, signifying the primacy of the eucharistic banquet, a foretaste of the kingdom of heaven.

Using mosaic, the central aisle itself will be a pilgrim way expressed in art. Imagery surrounding the font will depict the story of Noah and the flood, a vivid reminder of God's acts of redemption in human life. The Tree of Life, nourished at these saving waters, will spread its branches and mark the entire central path. Images of local birds and animals will be scattered among the branches of the tree. At the ambo, a depiction of the story of Jonah will illustrate the call both to preach the Word of God and to obey it. Finally, at the floor of the apse and surrounding the altar, the Tree will blossom with fruit, symbolizing the fulfillment of God's promises and the abundance of life that strengthens God's people as they come to be fed by him.

Above the altar, on the domed ceiling of the apse, a gleaming mosaic of Christ reigning in glory will oversee all of the action of the assembly. Thus, the most prominent architectural zone, which focuses visual attention on the altar area, will also contain the predominant artistic image.

At the same level, and running the length of both side walls under the clerestory windows, will be fresco images of various events in the life of Christ. This gospel narrative will move counterclockwise around the nave, beginning and terminating at the apse. Beginning at the east end, the north wall will contain images of the Epiphany, the Baptism of Jesus, the Wedding at Cana, the Calming of the Sea, the Feeding of the 4,000, and the Healing of the Man Born Blind. Beginning at the west end and moving along the south wall, the narrative will portray the Entry into Jerusalem, the Last Supper, the Crucifixion, the Resurrection, the Ascension, and the Day of Pentecost.

The sections between each scene from the life of Christ will be devoted to a procession of saints. A total of seventy saints, taken from the sanctoral cycle currently in use at the Community of Jesus, allows for a grouping of five saints per section. The current liturgical calendar is based on a consensus of observances of saints among some of the major Western denominations and on the desire to feature those saints who lived before the eleventh-century East–West split. Beginning at the northeast corner, the saints will appear in their current calendar order and thus will constitute a permanent record of the Community's calendar for generations to come.

Below these images, and sitting atop each limestone column, are stone capitals, each of which presents a set of symbols connected both with the artwork presented above and the liturgical action taking place below.

At the mid-point of the Gospel narrative, and filling the expansive west wall, one final image will be encountered before one leaves through the main door—the Transfiguration of Christ. The image will be portrayed in this appropriately prominent position in the church, for this is the Church of the Transfiguration. As an echo to the apse image of Christ reigning in glory, the Transfiguration stands as the turning point between Christ's ministry and his passion. Thus, it sums up both what he does and who he is in God's plan of salvation. This is the Lord who is worshiped within this place, and who is loved and served when leaving it.

At the date of Dedication, June 17, 2000, only a portion of the art work was complete. But the ground was firmly laid for the rest of it. In addition to the artists who have already been commissioned, the Community's own artists have been organized into guilds representing the artistic media planned for the Church of the Transfiguration: fresco/panel painting, mosaic/stained glass, sculpture, needle arts/textiles and calligraphy. Dedicated to the training of individual artists and to the broader promotion of each respective art form, these groups represent a commitment on the part of the Community to the future of these crafts.

GOD'S TROMBONES

In purchasing pipes for the new organ, the Community's musicians have often found it necessary to act decisively. However, even when one door has been closed, God has provided open windows of opportunity. This is the case with "God's trombone."

A few years ago, a call was received from the builder of the organ for the Church of the Transfiguration, with information about a set of trombone pipes, some as long as thirty-two feet! They would fit perfectly into the new organ, and they were available for immediate sale. So immediate, in fact, that a an offer had to be made within hours, as there were other buyers eager to purchase them. Within an hour, the decision was made and a bid was submitted. It seemed clear that God was providing.

The following day brought disheartening news, however. The Community's bid had been submitted twenty minutes too late. The pipes were sold and gone. Discouraged and frustrated, one of the Community organists took the unhappy news to the prioress. "Do you believe that God is in charge of building this church and this organ?" she asked. A simple but unconvincing "yes" was the only response. "Then," she continued, "if we are to have those pipes, they will come at another time, or something else will take their place. We need to trust God."

The following spring, the Community's choir was in the midst of a European tour which included Sicily. Awaiting them at the hotel after their early-morning arrival on the island was a fax from the organ builder: "The thirty-two-foot trombone has come up for sale again. If you are still interested, need an answer within 48 hours. Cheers!"

"Interested" was an understatement. Almost a full year had passed since the pipes had first been for sale. God had reopened the opportunity, and this time the Community's offer was accepted. The timing seemed to be no coincidence. A voice was being created for the new church, and it would include "God's trombone."

The Building Sings
THE ORGAN

For centuries, the pipe organ has been the instrumental "voice" of the Western church. Known from classical antiquity, its gradual appearance in churches sometime in the tenth century eventually led to its predominant use in liturgy, both as a solo instrument and for accompanying congregational and choral singing. Today, the organ's role is firmly established—to serve the church in the worship of God.

Music has been an indispensable part of worship at the Community of Jesus, and out of this has emerged a wealth of musical expressions. For example, Gloriæ Dei Cantores, the Community's professional choir, has amassed a wide repertoire over the years, thus requiring a versatile and expansive instrument for accompaniment. The design question became, Where should an organ be placed within an architectural style that predated the organ's use in churches? The apse was never considered an option because of its liturgical and artistic significance in relation to the altar, and the west wall was less than satisfactory, in part because of its distance from the choir and the rest of the assembly.

The distinguished organ-restoration and building firm of Nelson Barden & Associates, of Boston, Massachusetts, was hired in 1995, in anticipation of this project. Discussions between that firm, the architects, the consultants, and Community musicians led to a promising solution. The side aisles could house the organ which, when completed, will be large enough to be chambered down the length of both aisles. The space was not only available but also advantageous, allowing the voice of the organ to resound from many places throughout the church. The music might even "move" down the nave in tandem with a liturgical procession. The very building could sing.

The completed organ will include some 10,000 wood and metal pipes (the largest is thirty-two feet in length while the smallest is about six inches). It will integrate and expand several of the finest organs of E. M. Skinner, the preeminent force in American organ building during the first part of the twentieth century. Nelson Barden considers the organ's voice to be intimately connected to the human voice in its offering of praise to the Almighty. He writes, "Leather and lumber, wire and wind—if these things can sing with the angels, isn't there hope for us all?"

BY THE SKINNER OUR TEETH

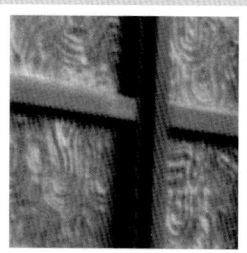

The first organ that would be employed in the creation of the church's new organ was a used Skinner, purchased in 1990. As is always the case when old instruments are rebuilt, some parts are functional, while others have to be discarded. The console of this used organ was in the latter category, or so it was thought.

Completely disassembled, the organ pipes and pieces sat in hundreds of trays and shelves for seven years, awaiting the day when they would be recreated into a new, whole instrument. The console, however, remained near the door, awaiting the day when it would be junked. As more pipework and parts were being acquired, space became more limited. Finally, the decision was made to take the console to the dump. But, on the day appointed, other jobs took priority and the disposal was never done. In fact, for many weeks thereafter, other jobs always took priority, until weeks became months.

The organ builder, meanwhile, was due to arrive for an inspection of all that had been purchased to this point. His own coming had been delayed as well, but the impending move to a new and larger storage unit brought everything to a head—his inspection and the console's demolition.

Over the years, the builder had been searching for a particular style of keyboard "action" made by E. M. Skinner. It was a feature both highly prized and highly expensive. He began to describe the touch of it even as he sat down to that old console on the day of his inspection. "You know, this feels like it," he said to his own surprise and everyone else's. Within minutes, the cover was off and he was lifting out a single key, under which was a small pin, no larger than a stereo needle. "There it is!" he exclaimed, lifting it up for all to see. "This is that rare Skinner action." Everyone stood in silent awe at the realization of what they had just witnessed. This very console had been long overdue for removal. How many days had it come so close to destruction? By God's grace, having "not enough time" meant having "just enough time" to discover that what was needed had been there all the time.

A Portal of Faith
THE WEST DOOR

The west facade of the Church of the Transfiguration features a central portal, the main door into the nave. More than simply an entryway, however, the large, unobstructed opening, measuring 14 feet high and 12 feet wide, symbolically represents the message of Jesus' own self-description: "I am the door; if any one enters by me, he will be saved, and will go in and out and find pasture" (John 10:9). Its sheer size is intended to highlight the primacy of Christ in God's work of salvation, while conveying the gospel values of invitation and welcome.

At the planning stage, the iconographic content of the door was determined both by what lay behind it, within the church itself, as well as by the atrium or "courtyard," which, following the completion of the next phase of building, will stand in front of it. It is conceived that, prior to entering the church and beholding the account of salvation, the arriving worshiper will first encounter the story of creation. The atrium therefore, will signify the opening days of creation, allowing the door to feature the sixth day, the creation of man and woman. Above the door and prevailing over the entire atrium space, will be an image of Genesis 1:1-2, the Spirit of God brooding over the chaos "in the beginning." In this way, all who enter this house will be reminded that they come as humble creatures whose lives have been given and are intimately known by the living God.

Adam and Eve are portrayed in a state of innocence and wonderment, as if arising from the freshness of creation. The shame of sin does not yet mark their appearance, though the shadow of its coming may be imagined, and even inferred by Eve's pose and expression. The tree of life at the center of the double door presages the imagery to be contained on the processional path in the center of the nave—the tree of life and its many fruits. Close examination of the doors reveals not only the fine detailing of the subject, but some additional complexities as well. For example, when the doors are open, Adam is seen gazing into the church, upward and in the direction of the apse mosaic of Christ in glory. Eve, meanwhile, appears to be looking out and downward, as if extending a maternal greeting to each person who passes through the doorway. Is that a note of sweet sadness in her eyes?

BE NOT ANXIOUS FOR TOMORROW

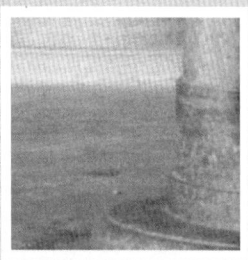

Raising a church of this character and quality requires raising money, and, in this case, both activities have been exercises in faith-building. Through the centuries, the sacrifices made by many ordinary people—offerings of time, talent, and material—have built churches in town after town after town. The realization of the Church of the Transfiguration has been (and still is) no different.

In general, the income toward construction has never been more than a month or two ahead of actual building expenses. Often, it has been less. But there has always been just enough to get through each step. Like the miraculous and daily resupply of the widow's cruse of oil, each time the last amount has been spent, funds have been provided from somewhere in order to take the next step. The Capital Campaign's director has a favorite story about one of those special times.

It was a day in August 1996, and the project was facing a financial crisis. Accounts payable exceeded $100,000, and the bill for the work of the previous sixty days had not even arrived yet.

There was, however, the possibility of a major donation. The situation was discussed with a donor who agreed to accelerate a year-end gift. Later in the day, the director learned that stock being held for this gift was now worth $101,000 and was being given immediately to the project.

But, as much as this story displays the faithfulness of God and the dedication of generous people, it does not end there. On that same day, another donor walked into the director's office, unexpected but quite welcome. Without a word, he handed over a check for $39,000. Later, in the afternoon mail, other unforeseen gifts arrived, bringing the day's total to $160,000! Those gifts fueled progress on the church for almost two months. More important, perhaps, they fueled trust in the God whose goodness and faithfulness could never be outgiven.

Worship in Word and Sacrament
THE LITURGICAL FURNISHINGS

The Church of the Transfiguration's long, rectangular shape provides for a main central axis running the length of the nave. Anything set within this path must therefore be worthy of such placement, for this critical location adds visual focus as well as symbolic significance. This is the case with regard to the baptismal font, the ambo (pulpit) and the altar. The prominent role of each has been expressed successfully through the careful wedding of architectural design and liturgical meaning.

Over the course of the design process, Liturgy Committee members made visits to dozens of liturgical spaces both in this country and abroad. Specific ideas were developed with regard to the form and function of these liturgical furnishings, as well as the nuances of meaning transmitted by each element of design. These ideas were then worked out in detail with William Buckingham and Dennis Keefe of Keefe Associates, Boston, Massachusetts, who created the final designs.

The Brothers of the Community of Jesus then constructed full scale models of the designs. The models enabled the committee to view various shapes and dimensions within the church itself, and to grasp fully the size and effect of each piece in its place. Artistic designs were developed by Helen McLean of Glasgow, Scotland, conveying the particular characteristics of each piece, while at the same time expressing their integral connection with the overall art program of the church.

In order to show the relation of the font, ambo, and altar to one another, the committee determined that these furnishings would all be fabricated from the same material. From among hundreds of stone samples, they chose Botticino marble from Brescia, Italy. This stone's beige color and golden veining would give the appropriate level of contrast to the interior limestone walls, while also adding a level of solemnity to each individual piece. Once the design and material were determined, Régis Demange, the resident stone sculptor, traveled to Italy to select the actual blocks of marble. Being a natural substance, stone varies widely, depending upon its source, sometimes even within a single quarry. Cranes large enough to lift 25,000-pound blocks were positioned to allow Mr. Demange to view various stones from every angle, and to test for cracks or internal imperfections in each block.

Two large blocks were finally chosen, and a determination was made about how each block should be cut in order to make the altar, ambo, and font. The cutting, as well as the shipping, delivery, and installation of the stone pieces, was managed by Castellucci and Associates from Rhode Island.

BAPTISMAL FONT

Symbolizing every Christian's initial "step" into the church, the baptismal font is positioned on the central path, very near the west door. Its octagonal shape can be traced back to many regions of the early Christian world, and represents the "Eighth Day" of creation—the new creation, time-beyond-time, eternal paradise. The font extends below floor level, a visual metaphor for being "buried with Christ" in baptism, and rising again with him in resurrection life.

The water in the font is made accessible for blessings as it flows from four bronze bowls, each of which is mounted atop one of the stone sides. Each bowl, bearing appropriate iconography, represents one of the four rivers flowing out of the Garden of Eden, as described in the book of Genesis. The font gates, which provide passage into, as well as a view of the water, are also made of bronze. Their patterns symbolize the power and movement of the life-giving waters. The same imagery is reflected on the floor of the font, in a mosaic designed by Helen McLean and crafted by Alessandra Caprara of Ravenna, Italy. The vibrancy of the colors and the repeating concentric wave patterns seem to burst outward from a central point, signifying the infusion of light and life from the regenerative waters of baptism.

AMBO

The centrality of the Word of God in the liturgy and life of the Community of Jesus is effectively embodied in both the location and the size of the ambo. It is the place from which the message of Scripture is proclaimed each day. Set as a great platform in the midst of the processional path, in a direct line between the baptismal font and the altar, it speaks of the necessary place of the Bible in directing and nourishing the Christian along the pilgrim way to God. Its proximity to the congregation is a reminder that God's Word is not far off, but very near, so that the church may "hear it and do it" (Deuteronomy 30:12).

A pillar of Botticino marble, standing at the west end of the platform, holds the bronze reading desk designed by Helen McLean. Through the use of a bronze "branch" rising from the floor and extending up the pillar, the ambo is connected directly with the mosaic Tree of Life as it stretches its way down the floor of the center aisle.

ALTAR

The apse has already been described as the visual apex of the basilica design. Under its dome, and standing as the destination of the processional path, is the altar. It is seen as a simple (though sizeable) pedestal with a monumental "mensa," or top. Its permanence is guaranteed not only by its purpose, but by its weight—the top itself weighs nearly 4,000 pounds. As the altar of an ecumenical community, it reflects both the "memorial" as well as the "sacrificial" character of the eucharist. Its stone construction and table-top design make it a blending of both of these traditions.

The top of the mensa is inset and incised with five crosses in the manner of Christian altars of antiquity. A Celtic weave pattern, emblematic of eternity, surrounds the north, east, and south edges. The west edge, facing the assembly, reveals two converging lines of six doves, processing toward a central symbol for Christ. Each of the doves, though similar, displays its own particular features, which represent the personal character with which each individual approaches the Lord. The design was conceived by Helen McLean and carved by Régis Demange.

Living Stones
THE COLUMN CAPITALS

Incorporating ancient Christian symbols together with items of local significance, each of the twenty-eight column capitals relates to the biblical scenes presented on the clerestory (the area directly under the windows) and on the spandrels (the triangular field directly above each capital and defined by the meeting of two arches). The main image of each capital faces into the nave. The sides and back contain related carvings, scenes from nature or from the local environment. In many cases, the capital images are also connected with the liturgical action that will take place on the floor level below.

For example, four of the western-most column capitals sit above columns near the baptismal font, itself a symbol of new life and spiritual blessing. On the north side of the font, two capitals depict jars of anointing oil and stags drinking at a stream (Psalm 42:1). Above them, the spandrels contain Old Testament images of David's anointing as king, and Naaman's healing in the waters of the Jordan. Portrayed at the clerestory level above is the account of Jesus opening the eyes of the man born blind. The two parallel capitals to the south of the font show doves, palm fronds, and a staff, over which the spandrels portray the anointing of Solomon and David's joyful entry into Jerusalem. The clerestory image is of Jesus' own entry into Jerusalem. In this way, the upper images "rest" upon those of the capitals, and all help to unfold a richer set of meanings behind the action of baptism which takes place below. Altogether, twenty-four of the capitals are woven into the overall art program in this way.

Four capitals sit atop pilasters in the east and west walls, at the end of each column arcade. Each of these capitals depicts a different archangel: Gabriel and Michael at the east end, Raphael and Uriel at the west. The angelic host is thus represented in their attendant roles, and, from the four corners of the church, watch over all of the activity below.

Like the interior walls and the columns themselves, the capital images are carved in Minnesota limestone from Biesanz quarry in Winona, Minnesota. The actual designs were developed by artists of the Community of Jesus, with the final full-sized cartoons being executed by Nadine Demange. Each capital was then carved by Régis Demange at his shop in Brewster, Massachusetts.

Called by His Name
THE CHURCH OF THE TRANSFIGURATION

Naming is a sacred act, for a name is more than simply a label of identification. It is also a symbol which carries meaning and value. It is a compact summary of nature and character—a recognition of what something is and a hope for what it will be. To name a church is an act of faith. It is both a confession and an aspiration.

In the process of naming the new church, two requirements needed to be met. First, the name had to be an expression of the biblical vision of Christ reigning in glory as the resurrected Lord. During Jesus' earthly life, there were only a few instances when his heavenly glory was revealed to the eyes of his followers: at his nativity, when the angels announced his birth and filled the heavens with their glorious song; at his baptism in the Jordan River, when the voice of the Father proclaimed, "This is my beloved Son in whom I am well pleased"; and on the mountain, when he appeared in transfigured splendor, together with Moses and Elijah. The name *Church of the Transfiguration* became an early consideration.

In addition to representing Christ in glory, it was imperative that the name reflect something essential to the Community's identity and the focus of its life. One of the professions made by members is the vow of conversion, the commitment to submit their lives to the transforming work of the Holy Spirit, and to cooperate as best they can with that work. This aim of personal transfiguration is part of what shapes the identity of the Community of Jesus.

Paul's letter to the Corinthians reminds Christians that they share in a divine vocation: "And we, with unveiled face, beholding the glory of the Lord, are being changed into his likeness from one degree of glory to another; for this comes from the Lord, who is the Spirit" (2 Corinthians 3:18). We ourselves are being transfigured into the likeness of Christ. Because of this meaning, which was further described by many of the early church fathers, the Transfiguration has taken a prominent place in monastic spirituality, particularly with its accent on conversion of life and communion with God. In his seventh-century sermon on the Transfiguration, Anastasius of Sinai places these words in the mouth of the transfigured Lord:

It is thus that the just shall shine at the resurrection. It is thus that they shall be glorified; into my condition they shall be transfigured, to this image, to this imprint, to this light, and to this beatitude they shall be configured, and they shall reign with me, the Son of God.

Five hundred years earlier, Irenæus had written:
To see the light is to be in the light and participate in its clarity; likewise, to see God is to be in him and participate in his life-giving splendor; thus those who see God participate in his life.

As such a formative theme through the history of the church, the Transfiguration is distinctly related to the broader church. Thus, the name gives further expression to the ecumenical character of the Community of Jesus. The feast day itself was observed as early as the fifth century, first in the Eastern churches, then spreading to the West. It is celebrated on August 6, and prayers are offered that our lives may be continually transformed into the likeness of Christ.

O God, who on the holy mountain revealed to chosen witnesses your well-beloved Son, wonderfully transfigured, in raiment white and glistening: Grant to us that we, beholding by faith the light of his countenance, may be changed into his likeness from glory to glory. *(Book of Common Prayer)*

CLOSING

More than ten years since it was first conceived, the Church of the Transfiguration stands finished, save for the completed art program and the full organ. It rises now as a house of God and a house of his people. In a sense, it is a testimony to the faithfulness of both.

The faithfulness of God's people has taken shape over these years in work and prayer and sacrifice. Some has been seen. Much of what has been given only God knows. Were it not for the dedicated lives of members and friends of the Community of Jesus, there would have been no dedication of a church. We, and all who have worked side-by-side with us, have sought faithfully to do our best, in the service of God, to provide a worthy house of prayer for the meeting of God and his people. The first letter of Peter is indisputably true—the church **is** built with "living stones."

But, when speaking of faithfulness, we are quicker to say that the finished work stands as a "stone of remembrance," a sign of the love and mercy of God. We stand humbled in the shade of its walls, for the church's very presence reminds us that God's thoughts far surpass our own. His purposes run much deeper than we can conceive. What good has been accomplished here is the work of God's hands, and our hearts beat with thanksgiving for the privilege of being stewards of such a place.

For the Lord is good and his love endures forever.
His faithfulness continues through all generations.

Grant us to be transformed as we behold,

O blessed Lord, this heavenly vision fair;

Your light and truth and love our souls enfold;

By grace may we at last your glory share.

From *Transfiguration Hymn*
Text: Hal M. Helms
Music: Michael J. Hale

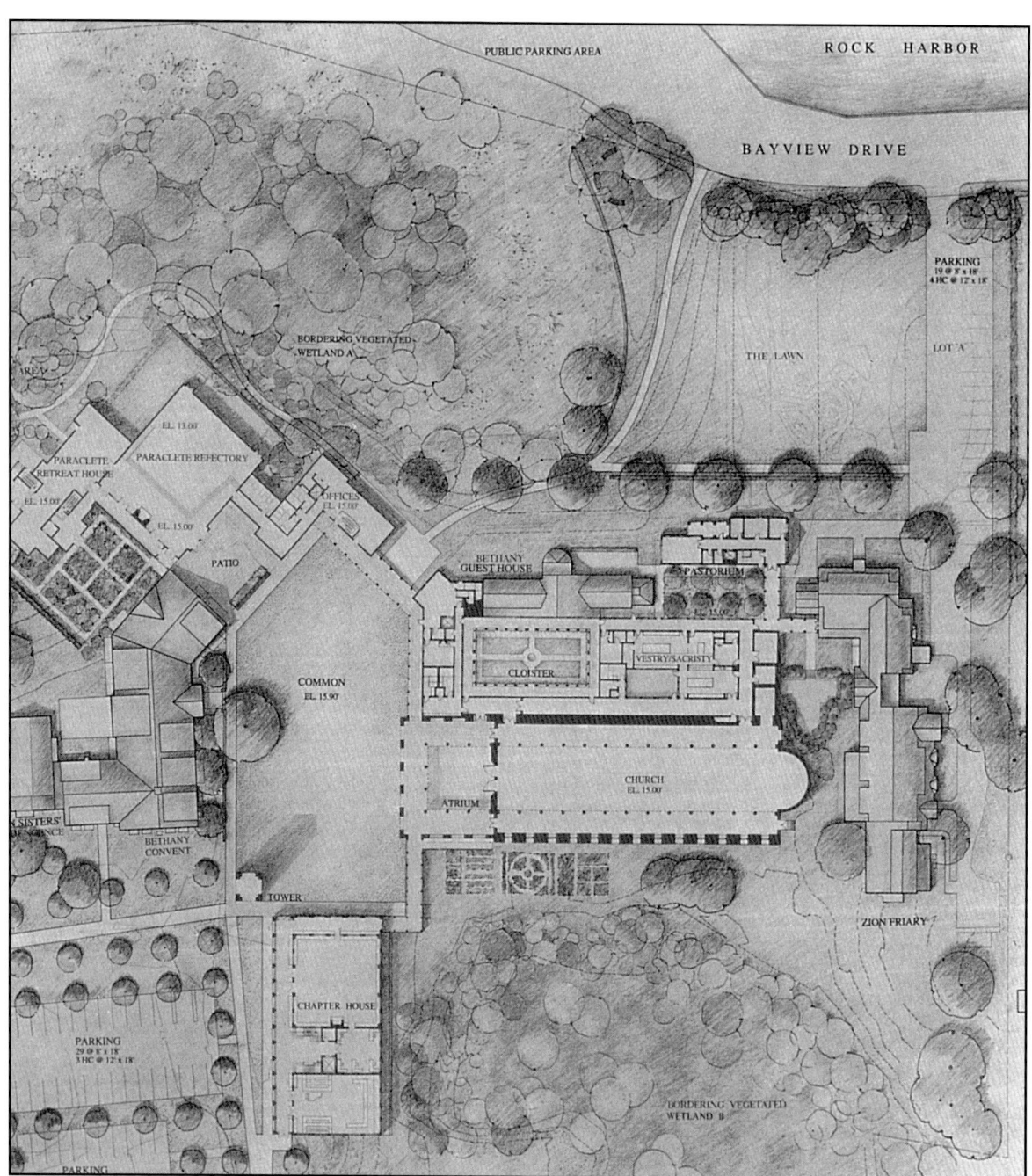

Epilogue
THE FUTURE OF THE PROJECT

At the Dedication of the Church of the Transfiguration on the Saturday after Pentecost, June 17, 2000, some six hundred guests joined the Community of Jesus in a festive ritual, the consummation of more than ten years of devoted effort by members, friends, benefactors and specialists. The door of the church was ceremonially opened to the exhilarating sounds of instrument and song offered in joyful praise to God. Both the building and the people were blessed, consecrated to the service of God.

As much as it was a culmination, on the one hand, the Dedication Ceremony was also a commencement, inaugurating the final steps toward the realization of the entire building project. For, since its initial planning stages, the task has been as much about building a community as it has been about building the church. Future phases will include the following:

COMPLETION OF THE CHURCH INTERIOR

Much of the interior art program of the church will take the next few years to complete. This includes the mosaics and stonework on the floor and in the apse, the frescoes at both the clerestory and spandrel levels, and the imaging of the Transfiguration on the west wall, which will also incorporate the round window. Installation of the interior stone will also be completed.

ATRIUM

A stone atrium, or open-air arcade, will extend westward approximately seventy feet from the main entrance of the church to the common. The atrium will be surrounded on three sides by covered porticoes, with a fountain set in the open courtyard. The artistic imaging in this space will connect with that of the church door and lintel, and will depict the first six days of creation. The atrium will essentially be a gathering space for processions into the church and for various liturgical rites which may best take place outdoors (for example, the annual Blessing of the Animals). In fair weather, it will be a friendly meeting place before and after services and concerts.

BELL TOWER

Detached but proximate to the church, a bell tower, seventy-five feet in height, will be constructed of the same Minnesota limestone as the church. Its design shows many characteristics in common with bell towers in regions bordering the Mediterranean. It will house twelve change-ringing bells, played by manually pulling a series of ropes according to precise and traditional patterns. Rising from the southwest corner of the Common, the bell tower will serve as a visual "gateway" and audible herald to the church and its surrounding buildings.

CHAPTER HOUSE

Formal, organizational meetings of monastic communities have traditionally been called "chapter meetings," after the ancient practice of reading a chapter from the rule governing each particular house. The Chapter House of the Community of Jesus will accommodate such meetings, as well as other group functions. Built of Minnesota limestone, it will connect with the church by a covered walkway, to provide ease of access between the two related buildings. This space will house common gatherings for various outreach activities as well as rehearsal rooms for the different musical and artistic groups that contribute to the Community's worship.

CLOISTER

Bordering the north side of the church, and nestled between Bethany Guesthouse and other buildings to the east and west, the Cloister will be set within this enclosed rectangular area as a place for individual prayer and meditation. The Cloister enjoys a rich and sacred tradition in the history of monastic life. The columned walkway around it (the gallery), and the open space within it (the garth) are designed to foster quiet thought and contemplation.

PARACLETE HOUSE AND REFECTORY

At the north end of the Common, a new Paraclete Retreat House and Refectory will be built proximate to the site of the former Chapel of the Holy Paraclete. Of wood-frame construction, it will provide the needed guest rooms and dining facilities for the Community's retreat ministry, theater space for presentations and productions, and much-needed work areas for Community offices. It will also house Priory Gifts, the Community's gift shop.

Architects, Artists and Consultants

for the Church of the Transfiguration
The Community of Jesus, Orleans, Massachusetts

ARCHITECT:

William Rawn Associates, Architects, Inc.

William L. Rawn, III, FAIA — *Principal, William Rawn Associates, Architects, Inc.*
M.Arch., Massachusetts Institute of Technology; J.D., Harvard Law School; B.A., Yale University

William Rawn has served as Principal for Design of the Church of the Transfiguration and the overall architectural masterplan for the Community of Jesus. William Rawn Associates, Architects, Inc., in Boston, has completed a broad range of work, from performing arts facilities, to college campuses and complex urban buildings throughout the country. The firm has won six national American Institute of Architects Honor Awards in the past seven years, including two in 2000, and twenty-seven city, state, and regional AIA Awards. Projects and writings have been featured in *TIME, Newsweek,* the *New York Times,* and major national and international design publications. Recent well known projects include Seiji Ozawa Hall at Tanglewood; music buildings at Phillips Exeter Academy and Lawrenceville School; concert halls for the Baltimore Symphony Orchestra in Montgomery County, MD, and the Santa Rosa Symphony in Sonoma County, CA; a K-12 school for the Walt Disney Company in Celebration, FL; and a masterplan for part of the University of Virginia. The recently completed Glavin Family Chapel at Babson College was featured in *Architecture for the Gods, Recent Religious Architecture in the Americas* (1999) by Michael J. Crosbie.

Douglas C. Johnston, AIA — *Principal, William Rawn Associates, Architects, Inc.*
M.Arch., Harvard University Graduate School of Design; B.A., Washington University, St. Louis, MO

Doug Johnston has collaborated as Principal for Design and served as Project Architect for the Church of the Transfiguration and overall architectural masterplan since 1994. His other major architectural and planning projects include the Phillips Music Center at Gordon College, the Northeastern University

Campus Masterplan, Dartmouth College Faculty Housing, Residence Halls at the University of Cincinnati, and the Cultural Center District Plan in Rochester, NY, featuring facilities for the Eastman School of Music. During his fourteen years with William Rawn Associates, Architects, Inc., he has led award-winning projects and has served clients from California to Maine.

ARCHITECTURAL COORDINATOR:
James H. Crissman, FAIA

M.Arch. in Urban Design, Harvard Graduate School of Design; F.A.I.A., B.Arch., Carnegie Institute of Technology

Jim Crissman's consulting experience, over more than three decades in the practice of architecture, includes cultural, educational, medical, and religious organizations. Representative clients include the University of Utah, Bennington College, Boston Symphony Orchestra, Harvard Business School, the Episcopal Diocese of Massachusetts, and Trinity Church, Boston. He is an active layman in the Episcopal church, and also an organist, choirmaster, and composer.

LITURGICAL CONSULTANT:
G. Thomas Ryan

M.A., The Catholic University of America; B.A., B.D., M.Th., St. John Seminary

As a Catholic pastoral liturgist, Tom Ryan serves as a consultant on the history of liturgy, architecture and liturgical art for the building of the Church of the Transfiguration. He has served as the Director of the Center for Pastoral Liturgy at The Catholic University of America in Washington, D.C., the Coordinator of Liturgical Architecture for the Archdiocese of Boston, and the Liturgist for the Cathedral of the Holy Cross in Boston. Tom is internationally known for his writings, including *The Sacristy Manual* published in 1993—the definitive sacristy guide for all English-speaking countries. He was also a syndicated columnist for national Catholic newspapers, and coordinating editor of the post-Vatican II edition of *The St. Andrew's Bible Missal*.

CONSTRUCTION:

John F. Kennedy, Kennedy & Rossi, Inc., Construction

M. Construction Management, Massachusetts Institute of Technology; B.C.E., Merrimack College

John F. Kennedy, the Chairman of Kennedy & Rossi, has taken an active role in the Church of the Transfiguration project, working closely with his project management and construction team. Kennedy & Rossi has been responsible for hundreds of projects in the New England area, with such clients as Massachusetts Institute of Technology, Harvard University, Tufts University, Genzyme Corporation, Cape Cod Hospital, Dana Farber Cancer Institute, Children's Hospital, Groton School, and Middlesex School, among others. Mr. Kennedy is a member of several boards, and is a lecturer at the Massachusetts Institute of Technology.

MASTER DESIGNER:

Helen McLean

Post-Graduate Diploma, St. Martin's College; B.A., University of Lancaster

Helen McLean was commissioned to design the floor and apse mosaics, the bronze work for the baptismal font and ambo stand, the stained glass window for the west wall, and the stone carving work on the altar, interior lintel, ambo, and west wall pillars of the Church of the Transfiguration. A native of Belfast, Northern Ireland, Helen completed her B.A. (Hons) in Fine Art at Lancaster University, and obtained a Post-Graduate Diploma from St. Martin's College. She undertook further studies and an apprenticeship in mosaic and stained glass in Sienna, Italy. Widely exhibited throughout Great Britain and Ireland, she has completed many commissions for large scale site-specific mosaic artworks, which have been installed in the buildings of private and public organizations. Helen resides currently in Glasgow, Scotland.

MASTER SCULPTOR:

Romolo Del Deo

B.A., Harvard College

Romolo Del Deo, the artist creating the bronze main door for the Church of the Transfiguration, is a Provincetown native whose tutelage began as a youth at the side of his father, the painter Salvatore Del Deo. His passion for sculpting led him to Italy, where he developed his art at the Academy of Fine Art in Florence, at the atelier of Rino Giannini, Professor of Marble Sculpture (Academy of Fine Arts, Carrara), as well as with artisans in Pietrasanta. Formally trained at Harvard (1982), he was invited to stay on "in residence" and instruct, while assisting sculptor Dimitri Hadzi in creating some of New England's largest contemporary stone sculptures. Currently based in New York City, Romolo is represented by galleries in both the U.S. and Europe, with a distinguished exhibition history and numerous national and international awards.

The design, clay sculpturing and finish work of the door was done by Romolo Del Deo of Brooklyn, NY, who also supervised its fabrication in bronze by Polich Art Works in Rock Tavern, NY. Each half weighs 2,000 pounds and is supported by a stainless steel interior framework. Certain steps of the intricate process, including the casting of bronze model maquettes and the rubbermolds for the actual full-scale sculpture, were produced by Pietrasanta Fine Arts, Brooklyn, NY.

MASTER SCULPTOR:

Régis Demange

Stone Carver/Cutter's diploma, École des Beaux Arts

A native of Troyes, France, Régis Demange was selected as the artist/artisan to carve the 28 limestone capitals for the interior columns of the church, as well as the altar and lintels. In 1985, he received his stone carver/cutter's diploma and another diploma from the *École des Beaux Arts* in France, with a specialty in sculpture. His career began with work on restoration and sculpture for several historic monuments in France. In 1993, Regis and his wife, Nadine, moved to California where he worked for a stone company, creating ornate fireplaces, pediments, and wall carvings. Currently, the Demanges reside in Brewster, MA.

MASTER MOSAICIST:

Alessandra Caprara
Licco artistico P.L. Nervi; Academy of Fine Arts, Ravenna, Italy

Alessandra Caprara has been commissioned to fabricate the mosaics in the floor and apse of the Church of the Transfiguration. A native of Ravenna, Italy, where she lives and works as a master mosaicist, she has been assigned numerous commissions from all over the world, including a replication of the "Madaba Map," an ancient mosaic map of Jerusalem, in Madaba, Jordan. She currently directs the *Mosaici Antichi e Moderni*, a well established mosaic studio in Ravenna, attends seminars and gives lectures in Italy and abroad, and participates in personal and collective international exhibitions.

ORGAN BUILDER AND CONSULTANT:

Nelson Barden
Nelson Barden & Associates, Inc., Boston, MA

Since 1956, Nelson Barden has been recognized as an expert and pioneer in museum quality restoration of electro-pneumatic pipe organs in the United States and abroad. In the Boston area, his projects include restoration of the renowned Aeolian-Skinner organ at the Church of the Advent on Beacon Hill, and the 118-rank E.M. Skinner at Old South Church, Copley Square. Currently, he is planning for the restoration of the Aeolian-Skinner at Symphony Hall in Boston. Mr. Barden tours throughout the U.S. as a writer and lecturer.

LITURGICAL FURNISHINGS:

William D. Buckingham, Keefe Associates Inc.,
Architects and Interior Designers

Julia Amory Appleton Fellowship for European Travel; M.Arch, Harvard Graduate School of Design; A.B. *cum laude*, Harvard College

William D. Buckingham is responsible for the design of the three pieces of fixed, marble liturgical furniture in the Church of the Transfiguration: the baptismal font, the ambo (pulpit), and the altar. Mr. Buckingham's projects have included building and renovation for the Roxbury Latin School, the Providence College Chapel, the Cathedral of the Holy Cross Chapel, and many others, as well as scenic design for the Loeb Drama Center and Lowell House Opera Group. He won First Prize: Visitor Information Center in Boston, MA; Honorable Mention: Rural New England Home Design, Washington Ridge, CT; and Honorable Mention: A New American House, Minneapolis, MN. He is one of eight architects on staff at Keefe Associates Inc.

LANDSCAPE ARCHITECT:

Susan Child, Child Associates, Inc.

M. of Landscape Arch., Harvard University Graduate School of Design; Certification in Landscape and Environmental Design, Radcliffe Institute, Cambridge; MA, B.A., Vassar College, Poughkeepsie, NY

Since its founding in 1985, Child Associates, Inc., has established itself as one of the leading firms in Landscape Architecture for private homes, private institutions, academic communities, and public agencies. Susan won national recognition for her landscape design of Battery Park City's South Cove Park in New York City. With her extensive experience and knowledge of all areas of landscape design and execution, Susan is an excellent project design consultant, lecturer and speaker, author and critic. She is currently the President and Principal of Child Associates, Inc., and a member of the Boston Civic Design Commission.

ACOUSTICIAN:

R. Lawrence Kirkegaard, Kirkegaard & Associates

M. Arch., Harvard Graduate School of Design; courses in acoustics and lighting, Massachusetts Institute of Technology;

A.B. *cum laude*, Harvard College

Mr. Kirkegaard has consulted on acoustical design in theaters, churches, and other buildings worldwide, including the Boston Symphony's Seiji Ozawa Hall at Tanglewood, New England Conservatory's Jordan Hall, the Wang Center, Carnegie Hall, and Chicago's Orchestra Hall. Kirkegaard & Associates has been a design partner in over 50 award winning projects, including the American Institute of Architects National Honor Award, National Merit Awards, Distinguished Building Award, and many others. He is currently the Principal Consultant of Kirkegaard & Associates.

STONE:

Biesanz Stone Company, Inc., Winona, MN

The Biesanz Stone Company is the source of the limestone used in the building of the Church of the Transfiguration. The company was formed shortly after the Civil War, in response to a growing demand for limestone in city construction. For more than a century, Biesanz Stone Company has provided natural stone products for both residential and commercial applications. These include floor tile, sills, coping, wall panels, and split face veneer, as well as a variety of other applications.

TIMBER FRAMERS:
Benson Woodworking Company, Alstead Center, NH

Benson Woodworking Company provided the timbers for the roof and ceiling of the Church of the Transfiguration. For more than 25 years, Benson Woodworking Company, a group of designers, engineers, business and craftspeople, has vigorously pursued an ambitious approach to building fine timber frame structures. The company has developed a reputation for integrity of structure, inspired design, and the highest standards of materials and craftsmanship.

LIGHTING CONSULTANTS:
Adam S. Kibbe, Ripman Lighting Consultants
B.A., Harvard College

Adam Kibbe joined Ripman Lighting Consultants in 1987, and since that time has been responsible for the lighting of over 750 projects. The firm's work has won more than 80 awards for lighting design.